PLANTS

Izzi Howell

WAYLAND
www.waylandbooks.co.uk

FACT CAT

Get your paws on this fantastic new mega-series from Wayland!

Join our Fact Cat on a journey of fun learning about every subject under the sun!

First published in Great Britain in 2016 by Wayland
Copyright © Wayland 2016

ISBN: 978 1 5263 0099 7

10 9 8 7 6 5 4 3 2 1

MIX
Paper from responsible sources
FSC® C104740
FSC www.fsc.org

Wayland
An imprint of Hachette Children's Group
Part of Hodder & Stoughton
Carmelite House
50 Victoria Embankment
London EC4Y 0DZ

An Hachette UK Company
www.hachette.co.uk
www.hachettechildrens.co.uk

A catalogue for this title is available from
the British Library
Printed and bound in China

Produced for Wayland by
White-Thomson Publishing Ltd
www.wtpub.co.uk

Editor: Izzi Howell
Design: Clare Nicholas
Fact Cat illustrations: Shutterstock/Julien Troneur
Consultant: Karina Philip

Picture and illustration credits:
Dreamstime: Neil Lockhart 4r; iStock: knape 19b; AVAN-
GARD Photography cover, Ikordela title page and 13t,
Meryll 4l, meawtai99 5tl, Ashley E. York 5tr, Dimos 5bl,
Artens 5br, showcake 6, saiko3p 7, Kazakova Maryia 8—9,
Bogdan Wankowicz 10, LianeM 11, Aleksey Sagitov 12, yev-
geniy11 14l, Jiri Vaclavek 14r, T.W. van Urk 15t, Gtranquillity
15c, Volosina 15bl, fotomak 15br, wawritto 16, michaeljung
17l, Africa Studio 17r, Nataliia Melnychuk 18, Annaev 19t,
Nitr 19c, kkaplin 20, Kelly Marken 21t, Marco Uliana 22b;
Wikimedia: Christian Fischer 13b.

Every effort has been made to clear copyright.
Should there be any inadvertent omission,
please apply to the publisher for rectification.

The author, Izzi Howell, is a writer and editor specialising in children's educational publishing.

The consultant, Karina Philip, is a teacher and a primary literacy consultant with an MA in creative writing.

FACT CAT FACT

There is a question for you to answer on most spreads in this book. You can check your answers on page 24.

CONTENTS

WHAT ARE PLANTS?

Plants are living things. Like animals and humans, they need food and water. They grow taller and bigger and **reproduce** to make new plants.

algae

Plants come in many sizes, from tall trees to tiny green algae. Find out the name of the tallest type of tree.

FACT CAT FACT

Some types of algae are so small that they can only be seen through a **microscope**!

Plants grow in many **habitats** around the world. Plants are often different from one habitat to another.

Spiky cactuses grow in dry deserts.

There are many types of brightly coloured flower in the rainforest.

Slimy seaweed is found in seas and oceans.

Plants that don't need much light, such as ferns, grow on the shady woodland floor.

PARTS OF A PLANT

leaves

stem

roots

Most plants have three main parts – the roots, the stem and the leaves. Each part of the plant has a different job.

Plant roots grow underground in the soil. The stem and the leaves grow above ground. What word do we use for the stem of a tree?

Plant roots take in water and **nutrients** from the soil. This water travels up the plant stem to the leaves.

The job of the leaves is to make food for the plant (see page 16).

FACT CAT FACT

Plant roots are very strong. Some can even break through stone and concrete!

LIFE CYCLE

The life cycle of a plant can last a few months or hundreds of years. This drawing shows the life cycle of a **flowering** plant – the dandelion.

1. A seed lands in the soil.

seed

2. Roots and a shoot grow from the seed (see page 10).

3. The stem and leaves grow.

The life cycle of a dandelion can last for several years. It will release seeds several times before it dies. However, some plants, such as sunflowers, only release seeds once before they die.

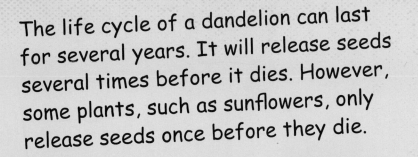

5. The plant releases its seeds (see page 15).

flower

4. The flowers on the adult plant make seeds (see page 14).

FACT CAT FACT

The life cycles of most flowering plants follow the seasons. In spring, they grow from seeds. Their flowers bloom in summer and their seeds develop in autumn. What happens to most seeds during the winter?

SEEDS AND BULBS

Most plants grow from seeds. When a seed is in a dark, warm, **damp** place, its hard shell breaks open and it sprouts roots and a shoot.

This is how a bean plant grows from a seed. Its roots grow down into the soil and its shoot grows up and out of the soil.

Some plants don't grow from seeds.
Plants such as daffodils and tulips
grow from a type of round root, called
a bulb. Bulbs are filled with food, which
the plant uses to grow new leaves.

Bulbs are usually
planted in autumn
or winter. In which
season will their roots
and shoots grow?

FACT CAT FACT

Onions and garlic
grow from bulbs.

FLOWERS

petals

pollen

There is pollen on the brown parts in the centre of these flowers, which are called lilies.

Flowers have petals around the outside and a powder called **pollen** in the centre. Most flowers need pollen from other plants to make seeds. Insects, animals and the wind carry pollen from one flower to another.

Flowers often have a strong smell or brightly coloured petals to **attract** insects. Some are filled with **nectar**, a sweet **liquid** that insects like to drink.

This honey bee picks up pollen on its legs when it lands on a flower to drink nectar. It then carries this pollen to the next plant.

FACT CAT FACT

The watermeal plant has the smallest flowers in the world. 5,000 watermeal flowers could fit inside a thimble!

watermeal

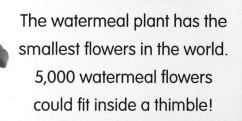

13

FRUIT AND SEED PODS

Once a flower has been **pollinated**, its petals drop off. A fruit or a seed pod, filled with seeds, grows in its place.

seed pod

Poppy seeds grow inside seed pods.

A poppy seed pod with thousands of seeds inside.

Seeds are **scattered** by the wind and by animals. If all of a plant's seeds grew next to each other, there wouldn't be enough space, light or water for them to survive.

When animals eat fruit, the plant seeds pass through their body and come out in their droppings. What is another way that animals can spread seeds?

Dandelion seeds have strands of hair that help them to float in the air and be carried by the wind.

FACT CAT FACT

palm tree

coconut

Coconuts, the seeds of the palm tree, are spread by water. Palm trees often grow on beaches and so coconuts fall into the sea. They are carried to different beaches where new palm trees grow.

MAKING FOOD

Plants make their own food using water, energy from the Sun and a **gas** called carbon dioxide. This happens in the leaves of the plant.

The process of plants making their own food is called photosynthesis (say fo-toe-sin-thuh-sis).

oxygen

carbon dioxide

water

FACT CAT FACT

Plants make a gas called **oxygen** during photosynthesis. Animals need to breathe oxygen to survive.

Plants die without sunlight and water because they are not able to make food. If you have plants in your house, it's important to water them and keep them in a sunny place.

Which of these plants gets plenty of sunlight and water? How can you tell?

PLANTS AS FOOD

Plants are an important **source** of food for many animals. Animals that only eat plants are called **herbivores**. **Omnivore** animals, such as bears, eat plants and animals.

Goats are herbivores. A goat will eat almost any plant, even **stinging nettles.**

FACT CAT FACT

Most herbivores eat a range of different plants, but some herbivores only eat one or two types of plant. The giant panda only eats bamboo stalks and the koala mainly eats the leaves of the eucalyptus tree!

Farmers grow most of the plants that humans eat. They plant **orchards** of fruit trees and large fields of **crops**, such as wheat and corn.

Humans can only eat certain parts of some plants. Which part of the bean plant do we eat?

carrots – root

apples – fruit

spinach – leaves

UNUSUAL PLANTS

The rafflesia plant has the largest flower in the world. However, its flowers smell like **rotting** animals. Its bad smell attracts insects, which pollinate the plant.

A rafflesia flower can be up to one metre wide. Where do rafflesia plants grow?

Carnivorous plants catch and eat small animals and insects. They need extra food because they cannot get enough nutrients from the soil in their habitat.

The pitcher plant makes a sweet liquid that attracts insects. The insects fall into the deep pitcher and are eaten by the plant.

When a Venus flytrap feels that an animal has landed on its leaves, its leaves snap shut and trap the animal.

FACT CAT FACT

A Venus flytrap can trap and eat a small frog!

QUIZ

Try to answer the questions below. Look back through the book to help you. Check your answers on page 24.

1 Plant leaves grow underground. True or not true?

a) true

b) not true

2 Which part of a plant makes food?

a) leaves

b) stem

c) flower

3 How do flowers attract insects?

a) by making noises

b) with bright colours

c) by moving towards them

4 Seeds need to be spread around to give plants room to grow. True or not true?

a) true

b) not true

5 Plants do not need sunlight to survive. True or not true?

a) true

b) not true

6 Which type of plant eats small animals?

a) bamboo

b) pitcher plant

c) poppy

GLOSSARY

algae a plant with no stem or leaves that lives in or near water

attract to make something want to come to something else

carnivorous describes something that eats meat

crop a plant that is grown in large amounts by farmers

damp slightly wet

flowering describes a plant that has flowers

gas something that has the form of air

habitat the area where a plant or an animal lives

herbivore an animal that only eats plants

liquid something that has the form of water and can be poured

microscope a machine that makes small objects look much bigger

nectar a sweet liquid made by plants

nutrient a substance that plants need to get from the soil in order to grow

omnivore an animal that eats plants and other animals

orchard lots of fruit trees grown together

oxygen a gas in the air that animals need to breathe to live

pollen a powder made by flowers, which makes other flowers produce seeds

pollinated when a flower is pollinated, it has received pollen from another flower

reproduce to produce new plants

rotting describes something which is decaying and often smells bad

scatter to throw objects across an area so that they all land in different places

shady describes somewhere that doesn't get much light from the Sun

shoot a new stem or branch of a plant

source where something comes from

stinging nettle a plant whose leaves will hurt you if you touch them

INDEX

ANSWERS

Pages 4–21

Page 4: The redwood tree

Page 6: The trunk

Page 9: They wait under the soil until spring.

Page 11: Spring

Page 15: Seeds get caught in the fur of an animal, such as a rabbit, and moved to a new place.

Page 17: The plant on the right gets plenty of water and sunlight. It has healthy green leaves and flowers.

Page 19: The seeds

Page 20: The rainforests of southeast Asia

Quiz answers

1   not true – they grow above ground.

2   a – leaves

3   b – with bright colours

4   true

5   not true – they need sunlight to make food.

6   b – pitcher plant

OTHER TITLES IN THE FACT CAT SERIES...

Space
The Earth 978 0 7502 8220 8
The Moon 978 0 7502 8221 5
The Planets 978 0 7502 8222 2
The Sun 978 0 7502 8223 9

United Kingdom
England 978 0 7502 8927 6
Northern Ireland 978 0 7502 8942 9
Scotland 978 0 7502 8928 3
Wales 978 0 7502 8943 6

Countries
Brazil 978 0 7502 8213 0
France 978 0 7502 8212 3
Ghana 978 0 7502 8215 4
Italy 978 0 7502 8214 7

Habitats
Ocean 978 0 7502 8218 5
Rainforest 978 0 7502 8219 2
Seashore 978 0 7502 8216 1
Woodland 978 0 7502 8217 8

History
Neil Armstrong 978 0 7502 9040 1
Amelia Earhart 978 0 7502 9034 0
Christopher Columbus 978 0 7502 9031 9
The Wright Brothers 978 0 7502 9037 1
Edith Cavell 978 0 7502 9772 1
Emily Davison 978 0 7502 9770 7
Mary Seacole 978 0 7502 9854 4
Rosa Parks 978 0 7502 9771 4
Florence Nightingale 978 1 5263 0168 0
Samuel Pepys 978 1 5263 0097 3

Early Britons
Anglo-Saxons 978 0 7502 9579 6
Roman Britain 978 0 7502 9582 6
Stone Age to Iron Age 978 0 7502 9580 2
Vikings 978 0 7502 9581 9

Animals
Mammals 978 0 7502 9598 7
Reptiles 978 0 7502 9602 1
Amphibians 978 0 7502 9599 4
Birds 978 0 7502 9601 4
Fish 978 0 7502 9600 7

Geography
Continents 978 0 7502 9025 8
The Equator 978 0 7502 9019 7
The Poles 978 0 7502 9022 7
Seas and Oceans 978 0 7502 9028 9

Science
Food Chains 978 0 7502 9695 3
Seasons 978 0 7502 9696 0
The Water Cycle 978 0 7502 9694 6
Weather 978 0 7502 9693 9

WAYLAND
www.waylandbooks.co.uk